Practical Guide to Understanding Your Pricing Options

Price Your Product or Service for Strategic Objectives

Steven Imke

Produced in the United States of America

First Printing, 2016

ISBN-13: 978-1534684461
ISBN-10: 1534684468

KSI Enterprises
395 Scrub Oak Circle
Monument CO 80132

www.SteveBizBlog.com

About the Author

Steve's first foray into the world of small business came when he was an Invisible Fencing dealer. He operated this business on a part-time basis while remaining employed by a Fortune 500 company called Digital Equipment Corporation (DEC). While the Invisible Fencing business was not very successful for Steve, it was a valuable opportunity for him to learn important lessons about business in a relatively low-risk environment.

After ending his relationship with Invisible Fencing, he worked on a business plan for a new business idea and waited for the right opportunity to present itself. In 1994, DEC fell on hard times. Instead of bemoaning this turbulent economic tide, Steve capitalized on this opportunity. He quit his day job at DEC to found Horizon Interactive, a documentation and training company. In fact, Horizon Interactive became a vendor for DEC.

Over the next few years, Steve and his partners executed the business plan. The business grew to over $3 million in annual sales and opened offices in several states. Horizon Interactive's success drew the attention of Interleaf, a publicly held company out of Massachusetts. In 1999, Interleaf acquired Horizon Interactive.

As part of the acquisition, Steve was offered the position of VP of Operations for their services division. Under his leadership, Interleaf acquired two more businesses like Horizon Interactive. The company grew the services side of the business from a combined $8 million in revenue to over $32 million in sales during the next two years.

In 2001, Interleaf was acquired by Broadvision, a California company during the height of the dot com era. Broadvision primarily acquired Interleaf for their XML engineers who worked on the product side of the business. Needing to divest himself from the services business, Steve and a former business partner acquired the assets of Interleaf's service business and started IC Interactive. They operated the business for a few more years until they sold it in 2003.

Being a serial entrepreneur, Steve has started and still operates three different businesses. One of his businesses is focused on real estate. The second one is focused on oil and gas. His third business is a company designed to help high net-worth investors understand the ins and outs of investing in oil and gas direct participation programs.

Steve has volunteered his time since 2003 as a mentor for SCORE, a local organization dedicated to helping entrepreneurs. He has acted as their Chapter Chairman for several years. He is also an advisory board member of his local Small Business Development Center (SBDC). In additions to his advisory role, he also acts as a counselor for the SBDC since 2003. In 2012, Steve acted as the interim director of SBDC while they conducted a national search for a permanent director. Currently, Steve is the Entrepreneurship Director at Pikes Peak Community College and writes a daily blog about small businesses.

Steve is a flaming dyslexic, which has its good points and bad points. Growing up, he remembers undergoing a board of education evaluation. When asked to draw a tree, Steve drew a series of concentric rings. When asked about his drawing, he said the rings were what you see when you cut down the tree and look at the stump. These rings tell the entire life story of the tree. The evaluator told his parents he was not normal. He should be more like the other kids and draw the tree from the side view.

However, rather than conform to the crowd, Steve embraced his out-of-the-box thinking as an asset. The upside of being dyslexic is exceptional spatial awareness and problems solving skills. Dyslexics develop these heightened skills since they are forced from an early age to compensate for things they do not do well.

Being a dyslexic in school prevented Steve from becoming a good reader. Even today, spelling and grammar are not his strong suits. Academically, Steve struggled in traditional schools. When he graduated from high school, he knew that a traditional classroom education was not for him so he joined the United States Coast Guard to learn a trade. Graduating near the top of his class in tech school, Steve realized that he learned by doing.

Steve tends to be an overly logical person. He likes to explore, document, and measure nearly every aspect of a project to find out what works and what does not. He has a propensity to focus on understanding why things are the way they are rather than how to duplicate what others have already done. Once Steve obtains a reasonable level of mastery in a specific subject area, he internalizes the knowledge and moves on to his next area of interest.

Everything of substance Steve knows about small business initially began by him reading books, listening to audiobooks, or watching others. He internalizes the salient points, then rolls up his sleeves and puts them into practice in his own business. Once Steve perfects a lesson, he makes it a point to document it and then share it with others. He calls these "Sea Stories," leveraging his old Coast Guard days. In addition to sharing his knowledge, this practice serves to further solidify his learning in his own mind while continuing to grow his knowledge base. In this way, Steve has codified over more than a decade's worth of his small business knowledge in the various books he has written.

This process has served Steve pretty well. By the time he was 42 years old, Steve had reached the point where he no longer needed to work for money. Passing this income milestone has not only allowed him the luxury to spend even more time to ponder and digest life's lessons, but also the freedom to tell it like it is without the fear of losing his job. He proudly wears jeans nearly every day. He also sports facial hair to remind himself and others that being a nonconformist and not subscribing to traditional viewpoints has its merits for entrepreneurs.

Steve constantly reads and listens to non-fiction audiobooks about politics or business related topics. He consumes current events from a huge basket of news sources every day so he can relate their messages in new and innovative ways. After internalizing a message and testing new theories, he shares his new-found wisdom with people willing to listen.

Since 2003, Steve has mentored and counseled thousands of fledgling entrepreneurs through his volunteer efforts with SCORE and SBDC. He has volunteered his expertise to help organizations like ARC, a program which helps individuals with developmental disabilities.

As cliché as it may sound, Steve is at the point in his life where it is all about using his skills and knowledge to help others to succeed. Steve never expects anything in return, but simply enjoys the appreciation he receives from the people he has helped and lives vicariously through their success. For Steve, sharing his knowledge is akin to the feeling a billionaire might have handing out $100 bills to random strangers on the street. He knows that by sharing some of the wisdom he has accumulated with clients, he can often make a positive difference in their lives. Steve is not particularly religious so helping entrepreneurs is his way of giving back and making a significant impact on the world around him.

Table of Contents

Part 1: Pricing Strategies

Once you know the minimum price you can accept to meet or exceed your break-even, you are ready to price your products or services to achieve strategic business objectives.

Pricing your product or service properly is one of the most overlooked marketing strategies you can employ to achieve the business results you desire. In the next few sections we'll focus on several pricing strategies. By employing one or several of these strategies you can drive customer behaviors to meet your business goals.

Volume Discount

The cost to acquire a new customer, if spread out over a longer period, allows you to offer a discount on volume purchases. When you buy a magazine subscription you pay less the more years you order because the customer acquisition cost is spread over a longer period.

Other times the shipping and handling costs are pretty much identical, even for larger sized units, so you can spread out these costs over larger product volumes. The cost difference between a half gallon of milk and a full gallon of milk is only about 20%, even though you get twice the volume of milk.

Can you distribute customer acquisition and shipping and handling costs using volume discounts?

Loss Leader

As a way to obtain new customers you can offer your product or services at a price that is less than your direct cost. Cell phone companies offer new phones for less than the actual cost of the phone in exchange for an extended contract. Razors are often sold at a loss based on the idea that the razor is useless without blades, which are then sold for a healthy margin.

Products and services offered at a steep discount or for less than their cost are called Loss Leaders. Loss Leaders can be an effective tool to attract new customers or get customers into your store.

How can you use a loss leader to attract new customers?

Pricing by Units Available

It is my experience that no two people pay the same price when they book an airline ticket. The list price for an airline seat varies depending on the number of seats already sold and the closeness of the purchase date to the departure date. If an airline fears that a flight will have too many empty seats, they reduce the price to sell more tickets. If they are experiencing robust sales they will increase the price to ensure they earn the maximum revenue.

How can you use the concept of pricing by the units you have available to maximize revenues?

Pricing by The Day Of The Week

Anyone that has ever shopped for the best airline ticket prices and is flexible on their travel dates knows that flights are cheaper on Tuesday through Thursday and higher on Monday and Friday. Since most business people travel on Mondays and Fridays demand for these seats are high, driving up per seat prices. Since flights on Mondays and Fridays are often full, the airlines want anyone that can travel on a different day to do so. They price the other days more cheaply to drive traffic to these less traveled days.

How can you use the concepts of pricing by the day of the week to maximize revenues?

Pricing by Season

Businesses that have inventory often have a seasonality to their sales. Holding unsold inventory for a year to wait for the next peak season ties up valuable capital. Savvy business owners mark up prices when demand is high and steeply discount merchandise at the end of the season to convert surplus inventory into cash. For example, people generally BBQ in the summer and particularly during holidays, so BBQ prices are generally not discounted during the summer or around popular holidays for barbequing. However, excess inventory at the end of the summer is often sold at discount, or sold to discount outlets, to convert inventory into cash. After all, it is hard to sell charcoal briquettes in winter (unless you live in the southern hemisphere). Likewise, coats sell for list prices during the winter and are steeply discounted as the weather turns warmer.

Sometimes the price widow is not based on a season but is tied to a specific day. Christmas ornaments are priced to maximize revenue before Christmas and are steeply discounted after the holidays. The same can be true for fireworks before and after the 4th of July. Pricing by season does not only apply to product companies but also to service companies. It is hard to find landscaping work in the dead of winter or to teach people to snowboard in the summer.

How can you use the concept of pricing by season to maximize revenues?

Pricing by The Time Of Day

Many businesses have peak demands at various times of day.   Popular restaurants are generally full between 5:30pm and 7:00pm for the dinner rush. Many restaurants have early bird specials to drive customer traffic for those more cost-sensitive customers or for customers with a more flexible dinner schedule to fill their restaurant during less busy times of the day. Cellphone companies and airlines often charge different rates for Peak, Off Peak, or Weekend hours.

How can you use the concept of pricing by time of day to maximize revenues?

Pricing For Loyalty (Repeat Business)

Customer acquisition costs represent a significant indirect expense. Once you acquire a new customer you should implement strategies to keep them coming back again and again. When you fly you often have a choice of airlines that fly the same route. To encourage repeat business many carriers offer frequent flier miles that equate to perks, such as early boarding, or that can be cashed in for discounts on future flights. Businesses from liquor stores to sandwich shops frequently offer punch cards. Once you achieve the requisite number of punches or stamps you can trade them in for a discount.

How can you price your product or service to drive customer loyalty through repeat business and maximize revenues?

Pricing For Loyalty (Membership)

If a customer has to go to some effort and expense to join a club they often develop a sense of loyalty. Sam's Club and Costco restrict shoppers unless they have a membership, which they get customers to purchase up front. Good Sam's (a camping membership) allows members to get discounts at participating campgrounds while non-members pay the full rack rate. You can offer tier memberships such as Gold, Silver, and Bronze to equate to different levels of discounts and/or other benefits. This can encourage increasing levels of loyalty by creating prestige associated with the increased membership levels.

How can you price your product or service to drive customer loyalty through membership and maximize revenues?

Pricing by External Factors

Within a few hours after the September 11th attacks, you could not find patriotic items like flags anywhere. Even before the day was out there were secondary markets set up selling flags and other patriotic items for more than ten times their price before the attack. Many store owners were not collecting the price premium.

Supply and demand should drive prices. When external factors create unexpected demand, the savvy entrepreneur should adjust prices to maximize profits. If they don't, others will capture the premium by creating a secondary market.

On an unexpectedly hot day at a football game a cold bottle of water should be offered at a premium rate, while on a unexpectedly snowy day a steaming cup of hot chocolate should be sold at a premium.

Failure to adjust your price based on external events means that you run the risk of selling all your stock prematurely. This leaves your customers willing to pay more for your products or services, but with no real option but to buy them on the secondary market.

Often the time window to maximize profits is short and fleeting. Consider the Furby craze a few years ago. Stores had waiting lists and sold out of the product before they could get them on their shelves. Buyers lucky enough to get a Furbe sold them on Ebay and collected huge profits, yet today you couldn't give one away.

What process do you have in place to examine external factors that will affect the demand for your product or service? And do you have a process to maximize revenues when demand spikes occur?

Pricing by Status Factor

Contrary to popular belief, people are really not motivated by money. They are in fact motivated by status. More money simply gives folks the ability to buy more status symbols, which they can use to flaunt their status.

That being said, most people equate a higher price with greater status. We all know that a cup of coffee at Starbucks cost more than the same size cup from 7-11 or McDonalds. Sporting a Starbucks cup in public makes the owner feel kind of special, like he is a connoisseur of fine coffee, because the more you pay for something the bigger the status symbol it is.

A woman's handbag holds the same kinds of stuff and costs about the same to make regardless of it being produced by Wilson Leather, Prada or Coach, yet the price for luxury handbags is a order of magnitude higher.

Ibupropfen cost more under the Advil name than the exact same chemical product offered under the Kroger label, because the name brand product holds more status then the generic version.

Can you create the impression of an upscale version of your product or service that you can sell for a premium price to take advantage of the increased status factor?

Pricing by Limitation/Availability/Scarcity

Limited availability or scarcity is a powerful tool to create premium pricing. There is only one Super Bowl per year with only a fixed number of seats. Tickets prices rise to meet demand. Furthermore, there are only so many ads spots during the Super Bowl. Here again prices rise to balance out demand.

The Organization of the Petroleum Exporting Countries (OPEC) historically placed self-imposed limits on oil production to drive up costs.

Pricing your product or service to the relative need of the consumer at a specific moment in time is also a powerful tool to extract the maximum revenue from a customer.

Consider what a customer with low blood sugar would pay for your last candy bar, or what someone is willing to pay for your last generator during a blackout, for your snow blower during a major snow storm, or, my personal favorite, for a pay toilet at the Oktoberfest.

How can you create a perception of scarcity to maximize your revenue?

Pricing for Cash Flow

Small business owners often live and die by controlling their cash flow. Having a customer pay for products and services as they use them may not provide sufficient cash flow to your business.

Getting the customer to prepay for products or services can be the difference between surviving and dying. Smart tolls and gift cards require you to front-load or prepay and then debit the card with each use.

A slightly more advanced version of the prepay strategy involves bulk buys. Cell phone companies sell bulk data plans and charge huge fees if you go over. This forces customers to pay upfront for the largest plan they expect to use, even if it means buying a larger data plan than they might have otherwise chosen to ensure they do not get hit with very high priced overage fees.

How can you implement a pricing strategy to get your customers to pay you upfront or make larger bulk purchases for your products or services?

Pricing by Available Options

Sometimes you have a new product or service category with little or no competition and are free to charge whatever you want for early adopters.

When I had an Invisible Fencing franchise the sum of direct costs for a self-install kit was about $100 in parts and another $100 to cover the parent company's national marketing efforts. My indirect expenses amounted to another $150 per unit. Therefore, I had a breakeven of about $350. We sold the self-install kit for $750 in those days.

One reason we could charge a premium price was that we were a new product category protected by a patent. The other reason and the subject of this strategy was based on the customer's other options.

Our Invisible Fencing customers essentially had three choices: buy a stockade (wood) fence, a chain link fence, or our invisible fence. The stockade and chain link options for a typical backyard installation averaged about $1,500 back then. So even though our product produced high profit margins at the time, relative to the customer's other options it was a bargain.

Do you have a product or service that you can charge a premium price for since the customer's options are limited or alternative solutions are much more pricey?

Pricing by Customer

Each customer is different in terms of their needs and ability to pay. There is no rule that says that every customer needs to pay the same price for the same product or service.

Working on a government contract has more overhead than working on a commercial account. As such, the billing rate we used on government contracts was often higher to capture our additional efforts.

Restaurants, particularly buffets, often offer a senior rate because seniors generally eat less and eat earlier then non-seniors. McDonalds offers similar burgers on the "Buy by the Number" board to burgers on the value menu. Customers can order a la cart for less money. This pricing strategy weeds out the cost-sensitive from the less cost-sensitive shopper.

Car dealers are the masters of customer-based pricing. They display a high sticker price on the car window. During the test drive the salesman assesses the customer's price sensitivity and haggling ability to determine the final price they are willing to offer the prospective car buyer.

How can you price your product or service differently to extract maximum revenue based on the customer's need and their ability to pay?

Part 2: Pricing Concepts

Understanding pricing concepts like pricing at the margins and price elasticity are important lessons for the entrepreneur. In the next few sections we'll focus on several pricing concepts.

Understanding Pricing At the Margins

Most service and/or product-based businesses define their prices using a cost-plus approach. This means that they calculate the direct and indirect costs to deliver a service and/or to produce a product, aka the break-even price. Then they add a reasonable profit margin to cover the risk capital for their initial and subsequent investments in the business.

While this strategy might make sense in geographically isolated areas it does not take into consideration the fact that many services can be off-shored. Products and services can be produced elsewhere in the world, often for lower costs.

To explore this idea a bit more, let's look at fuel prices, a popular topic for the media these days. The price to extract a barrel of oil from the ground and ship it to a US-based refinery varies depending upon a huge number of factors.

In Saudi Arabia it cost about five dollars to produce a barrel of oil and ship it across the ocean to a US refinery. In some places the US it cost about seventy-five dollars to do the same that is why when oil prices fell in late 2014, most North Dakota producers stopped drilling for oil.

Lots of factors contribute to this cost differential, including cost of labor, material, depth of extraction, and so on. But what is important to understand is that if the entire world's demand for oil could be met by the "cheap to produce" Saudi Arabian oil sources alone, the margin cost for a barrel of oil would drop to five dollars per barrel and producers with higher cost structures, such as those in the US, would be kept out of the market.

However, as global demand exceeds the supply of cheap to produce oil, whether the supply is physically restricted by production costs or strategically restricted by self-imposed OPEC supply limits, the margin price rises until demand is met. That margin price was about one hundred dollars per barrel in 2014 and dropped to just fifty dollars per barrel during 2015 to meet the world's demand.

At one hundred dollars per barrel, a US-based company that can produce a barrel of oil for a cost of seventy five dollars per barrel can make twenty five dollars per barrel. A Saudi Arabia-based company can make ninety-five dollars per barrel: nearly four times as much profit in terms of real dollars on the same product. This gives Saudi Arabia and other countries/companies with lower cost structures considerable power and influence in the oil industry.

So when Saudi Arabia wanted to stop the US from producing oil from more expensive sources like shale, it simply rose the production limits of its cheap oil and the margin price dropped to a point were it was not longer economical to many US producer to drill for oil in shale.

Margin pricing not only affects rising prices. but also

affects falling prices.

Consider how a new Wal-Mart store drives smaller business with higher cost structures out of business.

With the exception of a monopolized industry or organized union, unregulated market forces will bring prices down to the lowest level (the margin).

If prices in a particular industry rise, more businesses with higher cost structures will enter the market as the higher margin price makes it economical for them to do so. The increased competition will prevent prices from rising any further, reaching a sort of "price equilibrium".

Likewise, if supply can be met by either increased production capacity or lower demand, the margin price will fall. Then companies with higher cost structures will no longer be able to compete on price, and will likely be forced out of business unless they change their business and economic models.

Keep in mind that most industries are not completely unregulated. When providers or producers with lower cost structures feel at risk from new competition they often use their very high profit margins to protect their future profits by erecting barriers to newcomers or driving out competitors.

For example, they may contribute cash generated from

excess profits to the campaigns of lawmakers or Political Action Committees (PACs) that support increased regulation beneficial to them.

They may also support creating unions that control new entrants into a market, thereby placing a lid on supply.

Many factors are at play in establishing the margin price. A successful entrepreneur is one that keeps his eyes and ears open and takes stock of events happening around him. This is important not only to determine the margin price, but to consider the impact potential events could have on the margin price in the future and develop contingency plans to deal with them.

How would raising or falling margin prices affect your business's ability to compete? What events are happening around you that will affect the margin price in your industry?

Price Elasticity of Demand

What would happen if you raised your prices by 5%? Would it affect your ability to sell more product or services?

If after you raised your price by 5% you discovered that it had a very limited effect on sales, it would be said that your price is inelastic or not very elastic. However, if raising prices caused a large corresponding decline in sales, it would be said that your price is elastic.

In economic theory you want to continue to raise prices until a rise in price produces a corresponding decline in demand. If a 5% rise in price only incurred a 3% drop in demand, you are leaving money on the table and should raise your price further. By contrast, a 7% decline in demand would indicate you have gone too far and you need to reduce your price.

In actual practice the computation for your business would need to factor in fixed to variable costs. In essence, price elasticity is a measure of your customer's willingness, after a change in price, to either delay his or her purchase or search for a substitute product or service.

Have you used the theory of price elasticity of demand to maximize the price you charge your customers for your products or services?

Quality Pays

Often I encounter clients that want to produce a product or service on the low end of the price window in the hopes that lower costs will mean more business for them. However, being the low cost provider is not the best place to be unless your value proposition is clearly operational excellence. This is because unless you are the most efficient provider, with something like Wal-Mart's economy of scale, someone can undercut your costs.

In fact, your competition might very well come from an ignorant competitor that does not have a handle on his true costs, dragging your prices and margins even lower then break even. Also, lower costs often are associated with lower quality.

Remember, a person is ten times more likely to complain about a poor product or service than to rave about a good one. Bad publicity can cripple a business. Moreover, a person who paid $10 for a $100 product or service is more likely to complain that it didn't meet their expectations than a person that paid $1,000 for the same $100 product or service. That customer is more likely to write off the loss and just move on.

On the other hand, higher quality means higher profit margins, higher customer satisfaction, lower return rates, and less customer service and damage control expenses.

Is your business fighting to be the low cost provider, or should are you be focused on becoming a high quality provider?

Multiple Pricing Options

I often encounter clients that offer only a single product for a single price. Good marketers know that to generate more sales you need to offer pricing options.

Take your offering and strip it of all but the essential functionality, then price it at entry level price to attract your very cost-conscious customers. These are customers you would likely never have reached with your single pricing option.

Then provide your main offering, with all the bells and whistles, at a middle price point.

Then bundle your main offering with a few extras and price it much higher to act as a price anchor, making your middle price look like a bargain. The higher price may also snag the "money is no object" customers who only settle for the best money can buy.

A variant on this theme is to offer a "Freemium" version that customers can use for free either for a limited time or to act as an on-ramp to your flagship or pro-version.

Do you offer pricing options to potential customers to maximize sales and revenue?

Determine Your Hourly Rate

Most businesses are considered 'non-employer' businesses, where the owner is the the only employee of the company. Most are engaged in service or consulting industries and derive revenue via billable hours.

To determine your hourly rate we first start with the fact that there are 365 days in a year. Subtract from that 104 days to account for weekends, leaving you with 261 potential work days. Subtract from that 20 vacation and personal days plus 9 holidays. That leaves you with 232 days to run your business and earn your money.

Realistically, not all 8 hours of a standard work day can be spent working for customers. You will need time to devote to financial matters, reading email, marketing, office management, etc. Conservatively, these tasks will consume about 3 hours of your 8 hour day, leaving about 5 billable hours per day. 5 hours a day times 232 work days amounts to 1160 billable hours per year.

Next we need to consider your expenses. In addition to your wages there are the variable and fixed expenses of the business. You have to estimate your annual variable costs, such as travel costs, self employment taxes, franchise fees, etc. Variable costs are costs incurred only when you sell a product to have a billable work.

Now you need to account for your annual fixed costs, such

as rent, utilities, loan payments, phone, insurance, accounting, legal, etc. as well. Fixed costs are costs incurred regardless of a product sale or billable work.

Let's just say your variable and fixed costs account for $20k per year and you desire to make $100k per year. Simple math says that you need to charge an hourly labor rate of $103.45 per hour.

(($100,000+$20,000)/1160=$103.45)

Many clients recoil at this number, saying that the rate is just too high for the market. They vow to simply work more hours or reduce their expenses, only to miss their numbers and eventually either be forced out of business or work a ridiculous number of hours per week for a drastically reduced wage just to keep the doors open. Savvy entrepreneurs understand their costs and come up with down-to-earth expectations for the number of billable hours they need to bill to breakeven.

Is your hourly billing rate realistic?

The Drug Dealer's Mindset

As a business coach, one of the single most common issues I see with new entrepreneurs is their lack of understanding of gross profit, gross margin, and the impact of operating expenses. Their focus is almost always exclusively on the revenue gained from sales. I often refer to this as the "drug dealer's mindset."

Petty street level drug dealers are often fronted a bunch of product they are expected to sell for the distributor. As they sell their product, they are left with a fist full of cash, making the drug dealer feel rich and leading them to believe that being a drug dealer is great gig. Unfortunately, what the drug dealer has in his hands is called revenue.

Revenue is the result of sales and is not what makes you rich. A business needs to subtract their cost of goods sold (COGS) from their revenue to equal their gross profit. Gross profit is what is used to pay operating expenses, including wages.

The ratio of gross profit to revenue is known as gross margin. Gross margin is a much more important measurement of a business's health than revenue. The drug dealer sees the cash generated from his sales, but forgets that the cash is not his. From that cash, he still owes the distributor the cost for the product he was initially fronted or he risks "getting fitted for a pair of cement overshoes," as my dad would say. What the drug dealer is left with after paying his distributor is gross profit. Gross profit is what he can use to cover any expenses and pay himself for his efforts.

According to a study by the National Bureau of Economic Research, the typical petty drug dealer's average wage is only $6.00-11.00 per hour and many earn far less.

Many books on small business say that businesses live and die based on making sales. However, this is very misleading statement. Small businesses live and die based on their gross profit, not from sales. After all, I can always make sales if I sell my product or service for less than my actual cost.

Even big businesses struggle with this distinction. My business was acquired by a publicly held company during the dot-com era for our revenue alone. It was not bought for our gross profits, gross margins, or even the free cash we could provide. In fact, after the acquisition of my business, their business model doubled down on the "revenue only" drug dealer mindset.

After we were acquired we got new customers by agreeing to charge them less than their internal costs. We did this even if it meant our reduced price resulted in a tiny gross margin that would come no where close to covering even a small fraction of our operating expenses resulting in us losing money.

We only offered this reduced price if the customers agreed to outsource their entire departments work to our company. Since we were essentially giving away our services in the name of growing sales, it was no surprise that the division I managed grew from eight to thirty two million dollars in sales in only eighteen months.

Successful entrepreneurs know that it is not revenue or sales that count, but the gross margin you can produce from your sales. Without a healthy gross margin, your sales will not produce enough gross profit to cover your operating expenses and return a profit to the owners.

Do you suffer from the drug dealer's mindset and think only about growing sales or are your focused on how much gross margin your sales will produce?

Part 3: Behavioral Economics

Economics assumes that an individual provided with all the facts will respond rationally and make good buying decisions.

Behavioral Economics recognizes that our brains are hardwired in certain ways that make us respond, often quite predictably and irrationally, in ways contrary to logical economic rules. With a better understanding of just a few hardwired behavioral economic rules, small business owners will be able to achieve much higher profit margins.

Behavioral economics is a powerful tool that in capable hands can yield immense marketing advantages, resulting in greater sales and higher profit margins. In the next few days we will look at seven powerful behavioral economic rules every business owner should be aware of.

Power of Free

Remember when Blu-ray and HD DVD were competing head to head and it became clear that Blu-ray was going to emerge as the standard? Savvy retailers, knowing that buyers respond in irrational ways to the word "Free", began to offer HD DVD players that sold in the neighborhood of $400 a piece with "Five Free DVDs with the purchase of an HD DVD player". A rationally thinking person would say, what good is a $400 DVD player if I can't purchase DVDs to play in it? However, the irrational attraction to FREE caused consumers to clear the retailers' existing inventory of the soon to become obsolete HD DVD players, which allowed retailers to focus on the emerging standard Blu-ray devices.

Amazon recognized the power of FREE to tap into the irrational part of the consumer's brain when they began offering "Free Shipping" on items over twenty-five dollars. Now consumers often bought two or more items, though they likely only wanted one item when they initially visited the site, just to take advantage of the free shipping.

The word "Free" appeared in more then three-quarters of a trillion (not million or billion) goggle searches in the past month alone. Consider, "Free oil changes for life" if you buy a new car, "Free checking" if you open a new account, or "Free WiFi" if you stay here. These are just a few examples of how smart marketers have used "Free" to drive consumers into decisions that pure reasoning would cause them to ignore.

Knowing that buyers react irrationally to getting something for free, what pricing model involving something for free can you use in your business to improve sales?

Need to Compare and Decoy Prices

As a rule, faced with two similar options and one dissimilar option, behavioral economics says that most people will discard the dissimilar option and choose between the similar options based on our hardwired need to compare two like things.

Moreover, behavioral economics shows us that by contemplating a number, which in fact can be quite arbitrary, we can create an anchor point to set our price reference point as consumers. This is know as imprinting or arbitrary coherence in behavioral economics.

By way of example, consider the task of buying a new mattress. You see two pillow topper mattresses, one for $519 and the other for $540, and one memory foam mattress for $685. You have no idea what it will be like to sleep on any of the mattresses for a full night, so you must use other means to make your decision.

Enter the role of behavioral economics. The hardwired section of your brain that needs to compare options kicks in. You automatically discount the memory foam option, since you can't readily compare it to a similar memory foam product. However, its higher price set your anchor point. Your need to compare makes you focus your attention on the two pillow toppers. With little difference in the feel of the mattress you struggle with your decision, but finally choose the $540 mattresses.

Your choice of the $540 mattress is highly predictable based upon several behavioral economic principles. First off, buyers tend to choose the median priced option if presented with several prices. The high priced memory foam mattress served simply as a anchor decoy to drive up the price window. Next, your need to compare similar items forced you to focus on the two pillow toppers. You ultimately chose the higher priced option, in spite of the lack of a definitive difference in feel, based on your hardwired propensity towards products priced in the middle of the pack.

Next time you are out for dinner at a nice restaurant look over a menu. See if you can find that high priced decoy item and recognize how it makes the rest of the overall higher priced menu items look pretty cheap by comparison.

Knowing that buyers can be anchored by a high priced decoy and have an irrational need to choose between two similar products or services, how can you design your companies' offerings to take advantage of these behaviors and drive sales to specific products or services you want to move for higher margins?

Keeping Options Open and Fear of Loss

It is a good bet that when you bought your last desktop computer you choose one that provided you the option to upgrade down the road so you could keep up with technology. However, if you are like most people you never did upgrade, even though you payed dearly for the option to do so.

For many years I maintained an American Express card even though many places I shopped didn't accept American Express and the annual fees were high. After all, "Membership has its privileges" and I did not want to lose mine, even though I never could find out what those privileges were.

In behavioral economics we never want to lose our options. We often keep our doors open even if we never have any intention to go back through them. It is our often irrational fear that once we close the door we'll have the need to get back that prevents us from moving forward in a constructive way.

My healthcare plan is grandfathered in and if I choose another cheaper plan I can never go back. I'm not even sure what I might be losing, but the fear of loss prevented me for years from choosing a cheaper and perhaps better plan.

How can you use the irrational fear of loss and and a person's need to keep their doors open to drive up revenue and achieve higher margins?

Expectations and Price

A business associate of mine once used to charge $5,000 per day for his consulting service. I asked him once how he came to that rate and he said he heard someone was charging $4,000 per day and he wanted to be sure he was the most expensive option available. At the time he billed out about two hundred days per year at that rate.

According to behavioral economics he was banking on the power of expectations. With a high price tag his customers had the expectation that he was the best that money could buy, and they wanted the best.

If you went to a wine tasting and samples were provided in plastic cups instead of quality stemware your impression of the wine would be different, even if the actual wine in the glass was the same, because you had a different expectation drinking from a fine piece of stemware.

Tahitian black pearls and chocolate diamonds result from impurities and are considered to be inferior junk within their industry. However, great marketing campaigns make them appear to be rare. Raising these jewels' prices to make them appear more valuable made them very desirable.

Simply adding an elegant leather cover to a document or serving sandwiches on a silver platter will raise the consumer's expectation of the quality of the actual product.

How can you use the power of expectation to raise the value of your product or service?

www.ingramcontent.com/pod-product-compliance
Lightning Source LLC
Chambersburg PA
CBHW070412190526
45169CB00003B/1224